HOW TO BECOME A HUMAN RIGHTS PROFESSIONAL

- A GUIDE TO HUMAN RIGHTS ADVOCACY -

Copyright © 2022 by Isabelle Vladoiu

Editor: Olivia Flavell

Graphic design: AR Rajib

Published in the United States by US Institute of Diplomacy and Human Rights
www.usidhr.org

All rights reserved. No part of this book may be reproduced by any mechanical, photographic, or electronic process, or in the form of a phonographic recording, nor may it be stored in a retrieval system, transmitted, or otherwise be copied for public or private use—other than for "fair use" as brief quotations embodied in articles and reviews—without prior written permission of the publisher.

The author of this book does not dispense business advice, only offers information of a general nature to help you in your quest for business success. This book is not designed to be a definitive guide or to take the place of advice from a qualified professional. There is no guarantee that the methods suggested in this book will be successful, owing to the risk involved in the business of almost any kind. Thus, neither the publisher nor the author assumes liability for any losses that may be sustained by the use of the methods described in this book, and any such liability is hereby expressly disclaimed. In the event you use any of the information in this book for yourself, the author and the publisher have no responsibility for your actions.

ISBN: 979-8-42364-069-9

Praise for **How to Become a Human Rights Professional?**

"Compelling, Insightful, and Informative... This book is for everyone passionate about human rights! Whether you are just beginning or well on your way in the journey of advocacy, Isabelle imparts helpful tools to implement now. You will be inspired and equipped to champion social justice and advance your mission. This is a phenomenal guide on how to be an agent for change from a grassroots level and beyond." - **Blaise Hunter, Human Rights Consultant, Founder at Blaise the Trail inc.,**

"In order to realize our full human potential, we must first be made aware of all our human rights and fundamental freedoms... Thank you, Isabelle, for giving us the strength we needed to take the next steps toward Peace and Freedom." **Dr. Chaima Amari, Ph.D., Women's Editor & Advisor to PM to the United Nations**

*"I believe that we need to challenge ourselves to turn our resilience into our platform to be true advocates for all human rights, with the steps outlined by Ms. Vladoiu that you need to take to enter this fascinating and important field of human rights. You really don't have to be politically involved to learn about your human rights, so her book is for anyone who wants to learn more about human rights advocacy. Human rights are not just about the law; thus, human rights are non-discriminatory... meaning that all human beings are entitled to them! Thank you, Isabelle, for sharing with us a comprehensive guide to pursuing a career in human rights *Queen of Human Rights*"* **Nompumelelo Real Kunene MBA, BA, CTC, Human Rights Analyst - Swati Canadian International Corp.**

"I absolutely LOVE THIS BOOK! I learned a lot reading this. Human rights need to be recognized as more than a buzz phrase; they are grounded in our everyday experiences. We need to appreciate that cultivating a human rights and peace consciousness is choice-less: there is a moral imperative to engender and sustain an ethical praxis that is motivated by concern and commitment for how we live with each other. Thank You, Isabelle!" **Violeta Antovska, Diplomatic Security Officer to the Permanent Mission of Ghana to the UN**

DEDICATION

To all the dedicated human rights advocates in every corner of our world who are inspiring others through their work and teaching and who help promote peace in the world!

Special acknowledgments to my family & my fantastic team at USIDHR for their tireless work and dedication while I created this book for you.

TABLE OF CONTENTS

PREFACE 9

Chapter 1: Introduction 15

    What is a human rights professional?....................................15

    From human rights leader to founder....................................21

Chapter 2: The International human rights framework 26

    Definitions of human rights...26

    Human rights vs. civil rights and other types of rights...........33

    Human Rights vs. Civil Rights...34

    Human Rights vs. Freedoms...36

    Human Rights vs. Civil liberties...37

    Human Rights vs. Constitutional rights...............................38

    Evolution and classifications of human rights......................39

Chapter 3: Activism and advocacy 45

    Am I an activist or advocate?...45

    Is being an activist a bad thing?..47

    Preventing human rights violations through advocacy..........48

Chapter 4: Human rights education 51

    Promote peace with education..51

Empower the youth 53

Human Rights Education Case Studies 56

Chapter 5: Creating leadership through NGO advocacy 60

Becoming an NGO leader 60

What is an NGO? 61

The need for NGOs 63

Creating your own NGO 64

Chapter 6: Becoming a human rights consultant 71

What is a Human Rights Consultant? 71

Conducting assessments for businesses and delivering training 74

Chapter 7: Deliver human rights training 77

Why are human rights trainings needed? 77

What should a training include? 79

Chapter 8: Help shape human rights legislation 87

Legislative advocacy 87

Case studies 90

CONCLUSION 94

YOU MIGHT ALSO LIKE 97

BIBLIOGRAPHY 98

PREFACE

People can pursue many different careers, but few are as impactful and satisfying as working in human rights. Human rights are not just something people should stick to in the background. They're an integral part of our lives. The work you do to help others has real-world effects on people's day-to-day lives and can improve it depending on how committed you are. Think about the most impactful and satisfying careers out there. You might come up with some pretty impressive answers: doctor, nurse, teacher, environmental scientist. But one career that often doesn't get enough attention is working in human rights – and that's because most people see this as a hobby, a volunteer activity, or something that you do every now and then to contribute to society.

Human rights work is much more than just providing volunteer service to your community. If done right, this career can be both highly fulfilling and financially lucrative as well! And the best of all, unlike you thought, you don't necessarily need a law degree to become a human rights professional. The human rights industry is one of the few unregulated professions globally, like a bookkeeper, a financial analyst, or a life coach. Not to say that one can transform into a human rights expert overnight. It requires practice and knowledge. You'll need to demonstrate certain levels of skills and competencies. The human rights industry is a passionate and growing field that offers countless opportunities for those with the drive to succeed. With the demand for human rights consulting growing every day, there are plenty of opportunities out there. Companies want professionals who can help them understand how to make the world better for all - employees and customers alike. Meaning, if you know what you're doing when it comes to training others about human rights issues, this will hopefully be a space in which you can grow your career over time.

Human Rights work is a field that requires dedication and commitment. However, it's not impossible to succeed with the right mindset towards your job, especially when you're willing to learn from every opportunity available. The path to success is not a straight line; it's completely unique for each individual. But there are some commonalities that can help you navigate your way through your human rights career, and that's what this book is about! Even though this path may seem difficult at first glance because there isn't any "traditional" way for how someone becomes a successful human rights professional. Nowadays, we have more opportunities than ever before, simply because new technologies allow us access to industries previously untouchable.

The benefits of putting yourself out there are significant both professionally and personally. Attending human rights conferences, workshops, or seminars can help build your authority in the eyes of others while gaining knowledge on how to better oneself as an individual through these activities, which in the end may lead up to new relationships with potential employers down the line! When you want to build a career, finding people who will support and grow with your ventures is important. If you're searching enough, you might even find people who share the same goals as yours!

HOW TO BECOME A HUMAN RIGHTS PROFESSIONAL

Every day, people all over the world experience human rights violations. These can range from simple things like not expressing yourself freely to gross human rights abuses like enslavement and torture. If you're passionate about helping others, then a career in human rights might be right for you. This book will outline some of the benefits of becoming a human rights professional, as well as some of the skills and knowledge you'll need to succeed in this field. You will be able to go through it step-by-step, build your understanding of what a human rights career looks like, and get personal guidance about how I went from student to human rights leader and an award-winning human rights specialist.

Human rights are not just something we should talk about. They're a responsibility. And standing up for those who can't speak or defend themselves is one way you could bring your contribution as an advocate – but what makes this effective depends on how well-planned your strategy really is! This book will walk through all the different elements needed so there isn't any guessing involved, including tips and goals you must achieve. If everyone takes one step together for humanity, then our community might become better than ever before...there is no time to waste when human rights violations happen every minute.

You are continuing to read this book, and I appreciate that. The next step for us to succeed in showing you what it means to become a human rights professional is to make sure you take action, so please keep pushing yourself into reading further. It's important because when one starts their impact at the local level, it allows the effect to become increasingly widespread across other areas such as neighborhoods, cities, or even entire countries. If you're jumping straight from individualized education towards nationwide initiatives, you'll most likely fail miserably – which means getting nowhere… But by building your understanding of what this career is, step-by-step, one goal at a time, you'll learn how to create sustainable change.

When I started writing this book a while back, it was with one goal in mind: To give you the best possible advice on how to be a successful human rights professional. But writing it, I realized that one more thing stood behind my success. I am always the type of person that likes to be straightforward and give the entire recipe. I could not have published this book unless I also gave away the biggest secret behind my success - **and that is the secret of business etiquette and diplomacy.** For that reason, I first published 'Business Etiquette Secrets,' which became a bestseller almost overnight and has already touched the lives of thousands of people. So if you'd like to understand the entire journey that brought me to become one of the most respected human rights professionals, make sure you also read that book.

I created 'How to become a human rights professional' not as an academic book, but as a practical guide, so that you can always, at any point, go back and read any chapter when you require that specialized knowledge (more about that in **Chapter 1** of the book). Your journey in this book continues with **Chapter 2** and the International Human Rights framework, where you'll learn the definition of human rights, how we got from the rights of men to human rights, how to make no mistake about confusing human rights, civil rights, and other types of rights; and, discover the different existing international human rights systems. **Chapter 3** of the book explains the difference between activism and advocacy and whether you can choose to be one or both. **Chapter 4** then takes you on an exciting journey learning about the role of human rights education and how implementing human rights education early can impact decision-making. Next, **Chapter 5** reveals how to create leadership for human rights education through NGO Advocacy, how to start your nonprofit organization, and some of the best actions you can take immediately to ensure success.

This is crucial. NGOs are not just for the faint-hearted; they need people with passion and drive to make an impact on those who need help most of all. Most people open their organizations without considering how it could also be a business, successful enough so as to attract funds or build up teams – but don't think this way when you start your own NGO because there's no point in doing something by halves. Presented in **Chapter 6** is the road to a career in human rights; how can you become a human rights consultant? What are some of the key services that human rights consultants can offer in order to generate income? And because now you should have already gotten a better understanding of what a human rights consultant is, you'll get to learn what a human rights consultant does. **Chapter 7** tells you everything you need to know about delivering human rights training to others, from why they are needed to what a training should include. Finally, the last chapter, **Chapter 8**, shares how you can help shape human rights legislation in order to defend, protect and promote human rights for all.

So, if you're ready…let's start together on this wonderful road to becoming a human rights professional, and may you never be the same!

CHAPTER 1

INTRODUCTION

What is a human rights professional?

What does it take to start a career in the field of human rights? In this book, HOW TO BECOME A HUMAN RIGHTS PROFESSIONAL, I have outlined the steps needed to enter this fascinating and important field. From understanding the international human rights framework to the difference between activism and advocacy, creating leadership through education, NGO advocacy, and shaping human rights legislation, this book provides you with a comprehensive guide to pursuing a career in human rights. I'm not exactly sure what you were expecting when you picked up this book, but it definitely isn't the dry, academic tone typically found that will permeate its pages. In fact, this book is meant as a guide, something that you can always go back and read, and not a textbook for law students.

The language is simple, accessible, and helpful. So many books are written on the subject of human rights, tackling mostly their legal aspect, their sources, and especially violations of human rights. Still, not many authors have ventured to write about what it means to work in the field of human rights, leaving it a mystery to many. This book is not what you can find on the Internet but rather a guide for anyone who wants to become a human rights advocate and start their career in this field. It contains personal experience and analysis from a human rights advocate who has been there, giving you everything that's needed if you want to become one too! It provides a much-needed perspective that other books neglect because they are focusing more on legal terminologies or political implications without touching upon what it really means to work within this field day by day, the key activities that you are expected to do, and the knowledge you must have in order to engage in effective human rights advocacy.

This book is for anyone who wants to learn more about human rights advocacy, whether they are just starting or working in this field for years. I will walk you through the entire process from beginner levels all of way up towards advanced techniques so that everyone can impact their community and be successful at what they do! If you're just starting out in this field, do not worry, we will go through all the steps, from beginner to advanced. If you are already a seasoned advocate, but you're looking to learn more about how to help more people or grow your client list so as to create a bigger impact, this book is for you too because I am pulling off the curtain on the exact tools and the resources I've used to become a successful human rights advocate.

HOW TO BECOME A HUMAN RIGHTS PROFESSIONAL

If someone had told me ten years ago that I would become an award-winning consultant on human rights, I never would have believed them. But my calling was bigger than my plans. When I think about my life, two words come to mind: calling and preparation. Indeed, some might say that it's been a lifetime of preparation for this moment – I went to law school, I did my masters in international law, then I immigrated to the United States where I completed another Masters in Law, and now I am pursuing my Doctorate in Global Security. But actually, I took everything step-by-step, intending to educate myself more to be able to help others out along this path, too – for me, every career move was another door that opened up, revealing my actual purpose in life. Law school was not my calling. But one thing I learned is that you can't know what your true passion is unless it's lived and done.

For me, my passion ignited when I was very young. I witnessed first-hand the reminiscence of communism, born just shortly after the end of a 40-year era of communism in Romania. I grew up watching my grandparents, who lived during those difficult times and who were still in fear ten years after communism was over to talk about "important things" over the phone, afraid that calls might get intercepted. I was taught never to speak "badly" of the government because it could put me in jail. I've heard stories about dozens of churches in Romania that have been moved hundreds of meters away and hidden among other buildings so that they can restrict people's freedom to practice faith, as well as access to the only place where they could be themselves, under false pretenses about preserving architectural heritage. I've seen children my age come out to the playground very proud to have an orange, which meant only two things – they have rich parents or their parents "knew someone" that had access to imported goods, a rarity at the time. I've heard testimonies from my friends' fathers who've been imprisoned because they "dared to have long hair" and many more. That really woke me up because I couldn't stand to see injustices.

Then in high school and law school, I got involved in various humanitarian volunteer projects, from helping children in orphanages to visiting nursing homes, raising money for a charitable cause, fighting for freedom, and signing petitions for justice. All that experience gave me the necessary motivation to want to impact millions of people. I became eager to do more, and I understood that just by becoming a lawyer, I'm not going to achieve that. I've started my work in the community, meeting with anyone from children in elementary schools to community leaders and government officials, educating them about their rights. My passion for human rights education pushed me to apply to be considered to represent my country in the highest forums. Thus, soon after finishing my studies, I was chosen from thousand others participants to represent the United States at International Human Rights Summit hosted at the United Nations headquarters in New York. The opportunity that was offered to me was immense! Only 70 young people from all over the world were chosen to participate in this event, where I had to talk about my passion and volunteer activities in the community and share them with over 400 guests, including UN officials, Nobel Prize winners, and government representatives.

That day I realized that my work as a human rights advocate is never done. There is always more to be done and new ways to help people. I understood right there that human rights advocacy is a never-ending effort and I cannot and will not stop there.

Inspired by other young voices that I met at this Summit and driven by my calling, I returned to my community and as early as the next day, I started meeting people, sharing the new things I've learned and offered my help in teaching human rights classes for free to anyone interested. The community embraced my calling and dedication for spreading awareness on the Universal Declaration of Human Rights, and soon I've become well known in my city as I've touched the lives of many, from children to teachers, pastors, and leaders of nonprofit organizations. In only one year since I've represented at the UN, I've taken human rights education from the Buffalo Mayor up through county legislators, state senators, the Governor of New York, and finally, to the White House, and in 2018 I was recognized with the Gold Medal and President's Volunteer Service Award.

Why am I telling you this, especially in the first chapter of this book? You might ask. Well, because it's important to show how anything is possible!

And that belief has helped me more than anyone else could ever understand. I was young, I am a woman and an immigrant. New to America, with no family, friends, or close ties. But my calling and dedication were bigger than I could ever perceive. And that got reflected in the results, not in the medals, awards, and recognitions. But into the 10,000 children and adults that I've impacted through my teachings and human rights training.

From human rights leader to founder

In 2018, I founded the US Institute of Diplomacy and Human Rights (USIDHR) with the mission to help people and organizations enhance their global understanding of diplomacy and human rights – the two subjects I've worked on my entire life. Education can change the world, and creating my nonprofit was a means to help as many individuals as possible for one organization to gain access to education. Did you know that there are 258 million out of school children worldwide? This was one of the drivers behind the foundation of USIDHR, to give as many of those children access to their fundamental human right - the right to education.

USIDHR has grown beyond belief in such a short time with teams, regional directors, and volunteers being located globally. I'm very proud of our team's work to produce educational programs that equip people with the knowledge they need. One such course is the Human Rights Education Training, a certification program designed for those interested in becoming a human rights consultant and helping individuals and companies expand their understanding of human rights. More specifically, the purpose of the training is to help professionals gain specialized knowledge that they can then use to help organizations implement more human rights-friendly policies and conduct seminars and workshops to teach human rights, encouraging the circulation of human rights education. By teaching my students how to use the Universal Declaration as a moral code and how to teach each article of the declaration successfully, I was able to create an army of Human Rights Consultants. I will explain more about what it takes to become a human rights consultant, including an explanation of the various roles in which these professionals can engage in Chapter 5 of this book.

Up until now, we have certified over 3,500 human rights consultants in Washington D.C., the United States and worldwide who are making a difference in this world with their work - it's through them where I see the results of my efforts while also feeling fulfilled by them! My students have gone on to do incredible things, starting their own nonprofits, advocating for their causes with high-level officials, teaching their own classes, and even writing their own books. I don't need to convince you; I can let my students do that from the wonderful testimonials they have provided to entice others to enter into this career field.

'Today I attended your workshop/training on Human Rights and I thoroughly enjoyed it. Isabelle, you are articulate and culturally

sensitive. I love the way you presented and addressed the questions of our immigrant communities' **Ramon Sandoval**

'I'm really inspired and encouraged. This has been an awesome experience.' **Dr Anthony Spann**

'The world is in dire need of understanding and ensuring the basic God-given human rights of EVERY human being on Earth. This course delivers that message powerfully' **Dr. Gilbert Woodside Jr.**

'Such a masterpiece! It's a basic need for every human to learn and be informed about their rights.' **Alfred Agyakye**

'Easy to understand. Clarity and concept are phenomenal. Learned a lot from this course, now to move forward.' **Seli Moeai**

'Fantastic training for all mankind.. Do not hesitate to take this class. It's far more powerful than the monetary value itself. I absolutely recommend' **Bryan Lyson Theu**

'What an insightful and informative course!! I would recommend it to anyone who wants to upgrade their understanding of human rights. An amazing teacher as well.' **Eric G E Gaye**

'Thank you so much for making this course accessible. I have learned so much about Human Rights within just 2 days. This course is easy *to follow and understand. I look forward to educating others about their human rights and I look forward to the opportunities that this certification will bring me and others. I highly recommend this course; it is worth the investment! Thank you, Isabelle and USIDHR!'* **Ciera King**

'I concur with you that human rights should be mandatory to be learned in schools at all levels. The extent to which these basic rights are trampled upon or largely ignored, especially in political jurisdictions where dictatorships are still prevalent, is quite shocking; it seems there is no end in sight. It is therefore imperative that human rights education be part of the curriculum in schools from kindergarten.' **Itayi Marombedza**

'It's been great participating in this course and having the privilege to add to what I already knew to be The Basic Human Rights. I am equally very grateful for the fact that as a human rights Consultant, I have the tools and knowledge to advocate for others who fall victim to such circumstances.' **Fonderson Akah Asukwa**

'Thank you, USIDHR and our amazing instructor Isabelle Vladoiu. Spending this time with you, even virtually, was monumental and memorable. Lastly, you pour your heart and soul into this work and it shows! Excited to be one of your new

ambassadors in helping to educate others on their human rights.'
Natascha Saunders

'This training was an enlightenment for me and I am going to use it to make friends and families be aware of their basic human rights.' **Lion Shekee T.**

'I just completed the USIDHR Human Rights Consultant Certificate! It was an excellent and enriching experience. I will continue training with the USIDHR to better serve my community.'
Maria De Los A Hernandez De Casadio

'I'm so excited and feel so blessed that my dream came true, I can now say I'm officially a "HUMAN RIGHTS CONSULTANT." I am now able to help many people, thanks to Isabelle. You are a blessing to the world!' **Vicky Leyva**

CHAPTER 2

THE INTERNATIONAL HUMAN RIGHTS FRAMEWORK

Definitions of human rights

What are human rights? Before we build an understanding of the role that human rights consultants have in today's society, we must look over what human rights are. This question seems simple on the surface, but many people still don't know how to define them. I want you to take a moment right now and think about it yourself: How would you define human rights? Pose this question all of a sudden to any family member or friend. How did they answer you? What did they say? Do not be surprised if your friends or loved ones say, "I don't know." It is better for them to admit this than provide an inaccurate response. However, try asking the question again and see what happens! I surveyed thousands of people and trained tens of thousands of others in human rights. They all had in common that the majority were confident they knew the answer. But they were wrong.

HOW TO BECOME A HUMAN RIGHTS PROFESSIONAL

Too many people participate in presentations, take courses and read books with the idea that they already know what's going on. The truth is you will never get anywhere if your mind is closed off.

> *"It ain't what you don't know that gets you into trouble. It's what you know for sure that just ain't so."*
>
> *Mark Twain*

Understanding human rights can be confusing because they are not defined in one place. The field of law dealing with this topic is very diverse, and there is no single set of terminology for all the different ideas and terms. There are no one-size-fits-all definitions of human rights. This makes you think: Why should something so important only be taught in universities? I had to complete two master's degrees and specialized training in law school before coming up with my understanding of Human Rights. Still, we live in the 21st century - one shouldn't need an academic or professional degree for this knowledge.

International legal instruments don't always use uniform phrases. You'll find terms and notions such as human rights, freedoms, fundamental rights, citizens' rights, civil liberties, individual liberties, etc. An analysis of the content of the UN Charter, the Universal Declaration of Human Rights, the Charter of the Organization of American States, the European

Convention on Human Rights and the two covenants, the International Covenant on Economic, Social and Cultural Rights and the International Covenant on Civil and Political Rights reveals that these documents share in common the use of the term "human rights." However, they also use terminology such as "liberties," "fundamental rights," "fundamental freedoms," "rights and freedoms," "human rights and fundamental freedoms." For example, the Treaty on European Union refers to "fundamental rights of the human person," while the American Convention on Human Rights speaks about the "essential rights of man." The question is...are these the same? Aren't they just different names for "human rights?" I wish there were a simple YES or NO answer to that! But you'll have to keep reading if you'd like to get an honest answer to this question, finally.

I want you to know that I have studied for more than a decade to come to this understanding of human rights. I've spent endless hours studying and researching, reading international documents, and practicing human rights as a consultant. However, you won't have to do that any longer because you'll be able to find the answer on these pages. I'm revealing to you the secret of my entire life's work. Why? Firstly, I believe that everyone should know. It's time for all of us - no matter what country we're from - to have access to the knowledge of human rights without needing any previous experience of them whatsoever. Actually, there are a few reasons:

HOW TO BECOME A HUMAN RIGHTS PROFESSIONAL

1. It's my way of giving back to the world and helping prevent human rights violations from happening in the first place by educating people about their rights.

2. Because (unlike other "companies"), my organization, the US Institute of Diplomacy and Human Rights, is a nonprofit organization, and we believe in the gift of giving back to the community.

3. I get another one of our products in your hands, and when you see how awesome it is, it should get you excited to support our charitable cause. At USIDHR, we care about helping vulnerable children and ensuring they don't miss out on education by providing them with much-needed resources to go to school for an entire year. That means that all the funds raised from this book go to our Edu for Every Child program.

4. Finally, why wait for a change when I can BE the CHANGE? I firmly believe it is outrageous that in the 21st century, one has to go to law school or get a degree to learn about their human rights... so I thought it would be a breath of fresh air to allow everyone to get educated.

We need to look back at their evolution to understand human rights today. Examining the different terminology used in international documents from a chronological perspective, we can identify that in regards to the nowadays concept of human rights, initially they were called "the rights of man" (The Declaration of Independence, 1776) or "droits de l'homme" (Declaration of the Rights of Man and of the Citizen, 1789). In 1215, the Magna Carta mentioned, "No *freeman* is to be taken or imprisoned or disseised of his free tenement or of his liberties or free customs, or outlawed or exiled or in any way ruined, nor will we go against such a man or send against him save by the lawful judgment of his peers or by the law of the land." (Holt, 1992)

In 1789, the first ten amendments to the United States Constitution called the "Bill of Rights" introduced a more generic term, "the right of the people." (US Const. Bill of Rights 1791). The concepts codified in these amendments were built upon those found in earlier documents, including the Magna Carta and the Virginia Declaration of Rights (Mason, 1776), which highlighted that all men are equal. But the idea of "human rights" emerged stronger only after World War II; after witnessing the atrocities and murder of over 6 million Jews and others more, the international community came together to prevent such heinous crimes from reoccurring. The United Nations was formed, and the Universal Declaration of Human Rights (UDHR) was adopted on December 10, 1948, by 56 member states of the United Nations. The Universal Declaration of Human Rights is often considered the first document to recognize and proclaim "human rights" as we know them today. But an interesting story lies before this landmark act, which in my opinion, represents the critical moment in which human rights, in the sense we have today, were born.

Just a few months before the UDHR was signed, on September 28, 1948, Eleanor Roosevelt, wife of US President Franklin D. Roosevelt, who at that time was also chairing the Universal Declaration drafting committee, gave a monumental speech in Sorbonne, Paris, called **"The Struggle for Human Rights."** At the time, there was a lot of tension between states trying to agree on which rights should be included in the Universal Declaration and recognized by all as necessary. The problem was that they failed to come up with an answer because each country had its own understanding of rights. She mentioned, "There are basic differences that show up even in the use of words between a democratic and a totalitarian country. For instance "democracy" means one thing to the USSR and another to the USA and, I know, in France." (Roosevelt, 1948). As we previously described, up until that moment, the Magna Carta the US Declaration of Independence were all talking about liberties, freedoms, and rights of men. For these reasons, Eleanor Roosevelt suggested that the term' rights of man' be changed to 'human rights,' given the differences of what these rights meant to different countries: "...we here in the United Nations are trying to develop ideas which will be broader in outlook, which will consider first the rights of man, which will consider what makes a man more free: not governments, but man." (Roosevelt, 1948).

ISABELLE VLADOIU

Human rights exist to the degree that they are respected by people in relations with each other and governments in relations with their citizens.

Eleanor Roosevelt - Struggle for Human Rights
Sorbonne, Paris, September 28, 1948

This is a moment in history that not many know about. But now you do! There's now no way back to not understanding how human rights came about. As American civil rights activist Cesar Chavez once said, "You cannot un-educate the person who has learned to read. You cannot humiliate the person who feels pride. You cannot oppress the people who are not afraid anymore."

For me, this is the key to solving humanity's ills and building a better society. Having a complete understanding of why human rights are so important, why we need human rights, why we teach human rights, why we are so excited about sharing with everyone what they are, helping others understand, and raising their level of awareness. If you got to this point in the book, you are now part of the 10% of the world population with this knowledge. You're welcome!

Today, human rights are defined as those "rights inherent to all human beings, regardless of race, sex, nationality, ethnicity, language, religion, or any other status. Human rights include the right to life and liberty, freedom from slavery and torture, freedom of opinion and expression, the right to work and education, and many more. Everyone is entitled to these rights, without discrimination." (UDHR, 1948). Moreover, human rights are commonly understood as a given, as they are inherent to the human being and ours simply because we are humans.

Human rights vs. civil rights and other types of rights

Now that you have gained an understanding of what human rights are, you need to know the differences between human rights and all other kinds of rights. Going back to the exercise above in which I asked you to ask a friend or family member: What are Human Rights? You might have gotten answers like:

- human rights are the right to vote

- human rights are the right to remain silent

- human rights are civil rights

- human rights are those included in the Constitution

- and other answers alike...

Human Rights vs. Civil Rights

Are human rights and civil rights the same? Why are these two terms often used interchangeably? It's truly astounding how much knowledge there seems to be missing from our generation when we have advanced technologies, smartphones, and artificial intelligence; yet fail at understanding basic terms. A simple Google search not only will not reveal the correct answer but will confuse you even more. Here we are seventy-plus years after the Universal Declaration of Human Rights adoption, and people still don't know the difference. But don't worry! Everything you have learned so far from reading these pages has strengthened your knowledge. Human rights understanding is not revealed; it is built. Remember, it took me years of studying and hard work to know all this. What you've done so far has been collecting puzzle pieces, which in the end will give you a clear picture not only of human rights in general but of how you can excel in the oldest, yet the most unexplored industry as a human rights consultant. Just keep reading!

Human rights are inherent to every person as a human being. They are not something you are "given" or something obtained. You are born with them, and you have them simply for being a human being. Civil rights, however, are conditional; they can only be gained through belonging to one specific country or state. The difference between them, therefore, lies in how they're recognized. Civil rights are recognized by the government through laws or Constitutions, while human rights are derived from natural law and are universally protected and applied. To give you an example, in some countries, such as the United Kingdom, civil rights are protected by Common law or statute. In contrast, in the United States, they are protected under the Constitution. But does that mean they are different? Not necessarily. Human rights and civil rights safeguard against discrimination, injustice, and inequality. They are closely linked but not the same. The difference between human rights and civil rights stays in their number.

For example, in many countries globally, a violation of the right to a fair trial can be a human rights violation, but you're also denied your civil right. Also, the United States Constitution contains Ten Amendments that make up the notorious Bill of Rights. This protects a series of civil rights from freedom of speech, press, and religion, to the right to a speedy and public trial, and a right against unusual punishment. These rights can also be found in the Universal Declaration of Human Rights listed as human rights. However, the Universal Declaration of Human Rights proclaims the protection of 30 human rights. So what would you prefer to have? Ten civil rights or 30 human rights? Do you see the difference now?

It is people like YOU that have stood up to make a difference! Malcolm X, Martin Luther King Jr., Susan B. Anthony and many other human rights champions worked to recognize human rights by governments. That is why the more we raise awareness, the more we educate people about their human rights, the more the governments will recognize them and make these universal protections part of the law. So that in the end...all human rights...are civil rights! The question is....Are you going to contribute?

Human Rights vs. Freedoms

In addition to the term 'human rights,' there is also the one of 'fundamental freedoms' or simply' freedoms.' The two terms are often used together in international legal instruments. For example, at the European level, the official name of the European Convention on Human Rights is actually the "Convention for the Protection of Human Rights and Fundamental Freedoms." This raises the valid question of whether rights and freedoms are substitutable terms or not. The idea of freedom has been around for centuries. It originally had a collective character and was only recognized by cities or specific regions. The term was used long before that of 'human rights,' going through various transformations over time going from 'public freedoms' to 'freedoms,' and 'fundamental freedoms.'

Addressing the nation in 1941, United States President Franklin D. Roosevelt talked about freedoms, expressing that the respect for the rights and dignity of all countries should be the same as the respect for the rights and dignity of all Americans. Such respect was described in terms of four freedoms:

- Freedom of speech and expression

- Freedom of every person to worship God in their way

- Freedom from want

- Freedom from fear

What do you think those freedoms represent? Probably, when you think of freedom, the first thing that comes to mind is liberty. Freedom, in this sense, is the quality of being free. By ensuring that people have rights and that those rights can be exercised with dignity, only then will people have freedoms. In other words, it is the rights that help us achieve freedoms! From a legal perspective, though, the difference between rights and freedoms is almost nonexistent, and the use of the two terms together is more and more common.

Human Rights vs. Civil liberties

In addition to 'freedoms,' there is also the notion of 'civil liberties.' In the United States, according to the Nolo's Plain-English Law Dictionary, civil liberties are "rights granted to the people under the Constitution (and derived primarily from the First Amendment), to speak freely, think, assemble, organize, worship, or petition without government interference or restraints." However, civil liberties should not be confused with the civil rights that we described above (Sepuldeva et al., 2010). Some argue that the purpose of civil liberties is to "protect individuals from governmental intrusions on fundamental freedoms," (Domino, 2018) while 'civil rights' refer to governmental acts that "guarantee that each person is treated as an equal member of society." Civil liberties involve, therefore, both freedoms and human rights and are subject to a separate set of legal rules.

Human Rights vs. Constitutional rights

We discussed so far that there are a few different types of rights that can be found in a country's legal system. These include fundamental freedoms, which due to their importance, were included as part of declarations or Constitutions, also called 'constitutional rights' or 'supreme rights' for this reason. Fundamental rights are the private rights of citizens essential to their life, freedom, and dignity. These inalienable protections are guaranteed by the Constitution. In practice, fundamental rights mean such rights as the right to life and the inviolability of the person (Sepuldeva, 2010). Fundamental rights, therefore, are included in the broader category of human rights; however, they make the core of rights that belong to human beings. This means that without their existence, the term 'violation of human rights' would lose its significance. Also, fundamental rights are given priority in national and international policy.

Perhaps, even if you don't live in the United States, the following example is the best way to understand the difference between fundamental rights and human rights. The distinction between human rights in general and fundamental ones is of utmost importance to US Courts. Every time a restriction on one's freedom has been imposed, they will apply different levels for scrutiny. That means every time a law or a policy by the government limits one of the fundamental rights included in the US Constitution; the judge will apply the most stringent standard of judicial review. As part of this process, courts will decide whether a right is fundamental or not by examining the historical foundations of such a right. If it is agreed that the specific right has enjoyed protection as part of a longstanding tradition, the right will be considered to be a fundamental right. One important note here, US states are allowed to expand which rights should be included into their category of fundamental rights. Still, they should never diminish or infringe upon fundamental rights by legislative processes.

Evolution and classifications of human rights

The idea of human rights is not a new one. It existed in various forms throughout history, and to reach what we understand today as their definition; society had to go through many transformations. When it comes to human rights, traditional societies have always framed systems of duties with the concepts of justice and political legitimacy in mind (Donnelly, 2013). But justice and political legitimacy are instead alternatives to human rights than different formulations of them (Donnelly, 2013). Even as early as 1770 BC, the Code of Hammurabi regulated social relations and safeguarded rules for humanity. Also, the Law of the Polis was an ancient Greek law that promoted citizen participation in government and society. In ancient Rome, the right of

Roman citizens to participate in public life was recognized as an individual right to all Roman citizens.

Moreover, even ancient philosophers such as Cicero and Seneca in their works used terms such as "individual liberties' and "equality between people." The concept of "human rights' appears to be formulated for the first time in the seventeenth century in the philosophy of Natural Law. The theory of natural law (ius natural) was opposed to civil law (ius civil), the first applying to all people, while the second belongs only to the members of the fortress. The School of Natural Law proposed that humans are a social value in themselves and deserve to be treated with respect (Lochak, 2002). Jean Bodin advanced the idea of human rights by denying them, considering that the sovereignty of the king cannot be questioned by anyone and that he is compelled to respect only divine commandments, natural law, and the general principles of law (Vladoiu, 2014). Thomas Hobbes considered humans as selfish, starting from the Latin datum "homo homini lupus," meaning "a man is a wolf to another man." He proposed the idea of a 'social contract' where men would give up their rights to be able to be led. John Locke believed that rights such as the right to property, personal freedom, and legitimate defense are imprescriptible and inalienable, meaning they never end and cannot be taken away (Simmons, 2020). In his book, The Social Contract, J. J. Rousseau argued that "man is born free, but he is everywhere in chains" (Rousseau, 1964). In this sense, under a contract with the state, people transfer their natural rights, only to receive them back as civil rights

(Rousseau, 1964). Similarly, Voltaire claimed that to be free means to know your human rights, and knowing them means to defend them (Lochak, 2002).

The concept of human rights has therefore evolved over time and is now recognized as an international system. Their definition has been a constant concern for centuries. Still, since the end of the 18th century, this topic has moved on to another phase in which it transforms - becoming what today's society knows best: **The International Human Rights System.**

The above evolution of human rights can help you understand the complexity of human rights. As you saw, human rights have been widely used for centuries; however, there is no single classification system that is universally agreed upon. Instead, there are several different systems of rights that have their own set of rules. Let's go over a few of them.

Depending on the geographical coverage of their protection, there are:

a)   universal systems of human rights

b)   regional systems of human rights

This classification is based on the international legal instruments protecting human rights and not on the rights themselves. Examples of universal human rights systems: the UN Human Rights System and the

International Bill of Rights made of the Universal Declaration of Human Rights and the two international covenants - the International Covenant on Civil and Political Rights and the International Covenant on Economic, Social and Cultural Rights. Examples of regional human rights systems include the European Human Rights System, the African Human Rights System, the Arab Human Rights System, and others.

Depending on the beneficiaries that they protect, there are:

a)   general human rights

b)   specific rights

General human rights apply to all individuals, while specific rights are recognized for certain categories of people, such as women (e.g., Convention on the Elimination of All Forms of Discrimination against Women), children (Convention on the Rights of the Child), minorities (Declaration on the Rights of Indigenous Peoples), and many others categories.

Similarly, based on the same criteria, we distinguish between:

a)   individual rights

b)   collective rights - provided for the protection of the interests of a group of persons, collectively holding rights, such as minority rights.

Individual rights are those recognized by every individual, regardless of whether they are exercised individually or collectively. By comparison, collective rights are those such as freedom of religion, freedom of association or assembly, rights which are usually exercised by people in groups.

In terms of their content, there are:

a)   civil and political rights

b)   economic, social and cultural rights

Civil and political rights are those rights whose exercise ensures the democratic development of society in its political dimension. Economic, social, and cultural rights are those capable of leading to the establishment of economic democracy in society, such as the right to education, the right to work, the right to property.

In terms of their historical evolution, we distinguish:

a)   First generation rights

b)   Second generation rights

c)   Third generation rights

All the civil and political rights are first-generation rights. Social, economic, and cultural rights are second-generation rights. Collective rights, such as, for example, the right to a healthy environment or the right to development, are third-generation rights.

CHAPTER 3

ACTIVISM AND ADVOCACY

———— ◆◇◆ ————

Am I an activist or advocate?

If you've found yourself asking this question lately, you're not alone. We all know how frustrating it is when we have a question, and Google doesn't seem to be able to answer. In this case, if you're thinking about going down that road, then don't bother because you're just one step closer to being even more confused! When it relates to the human rights field, what is the difference between an activist and an advocate? Is there a specific type of person that only wants to be one, or can they overlap? If so, can someone act as both at different times in their life depending on what's needed for each specific mission?

Human rights are a universal concern. There isn't one single way to promote them, but there's no need for an exclusive label either; every person can be both an activist and an advocate in their own personal life while working on other related public issues. For these reasons, the terms' activist' or 'advocacy' are often equated with one another because they both work to promote change or transformation in society; however-the, the goals associated with these names and means to achieve them are often different or at least should be different. An activist is someone who takes action to promote social change. They're more involved in active pursuits such as demonstrations, strikes, and campaigns. At the same time, an advocate has a tendency towards working behind the scenes with legislation or policies that affect large groups of people. An activist's goal is to create an impact and make people listen - whether they want to or not. On the contrary, the purpose of advocacy is to convince others of your cause through dialogue. It often involves listening to their thoughts, making them aware of yours, and settling disputes through mutual understanding - just like in negotiations.

To be an activist is to speak. To be an advocate is to listen

Ewa Lewis

For that reason, becoming an activist is seen as something accessible, which you can transform into overnight, without previous experience, without finding facts or researching work, because what matters is to be passionate about a cause and to speak out for it. Youth are more likely than any other age group to try out activism at least once in their lives. But there's an eagerness for trying out at least one "experience" of activism for anyone regardless of age.

Is being an activist a bad thing?

In recent years, the word "activist" has been thrown around a lot and has been given a negative meaning. It's not just used as an umbrella term for people who are passionate about social or political issues, but also something that can be done with relatively little risk-taking compared to advocacy. But that is not entirely true. Activism does entail more than simply speaking up, as you're actively taking part in change efforts by engaging your voice through public protests. Making change is hard. It requires a long and often difficult road of collective action at multiple levels. Usually, advocates, after completing their education, work in producing change, are followed by activists who demand change. Yet, the case for advocacy is strong.

To be an advocate means "to publicly support or suggest an idea, development, or way of doing something" (Cambridge Dictionary) - which can also mean listening closely and understanding what other people need without necessarily taking on their perspective yourself; whereas to be an activist can also refer to somebody that makes noise when they don't agree with something, even though it's usually negative sounding. Why do you think human rights advocacy produces more substantial change? Advocacy is not only engaged after human rights violations occur; it can be used to prevent them from occurring in the first place. Therefore, it can have a much more profound impact on the future. By working towards preventing these issues instead of voicing opinions after they've occurred, human rights advocacy lays the groundwork for ways to avoid injustice.

Think of an activism campaign that was put in place to raise awareness about an issue, such as, for example, Justice for George Floyd, the #MeToo movement, Black Lives Matter, and many others. All these have been successful movements in terms of raising awareness and have gotten substantial attention from the media. The #MeToo movement has raised several eyebrows and started many conversations, but what did it really do? It's hard to say if it achieved significant legislation changes or even justice for all victims. However, it obviously produced some outcomes such as increased sensitivity, local legislative or policy changes, increased worker protection, etc. But while we can't disavow activism and deny its ability to incite a change, it does not radically change the injustices, prejudices, and cultural attitudes that underlie the issues for which activism is used in the first place. This requires advocacy. In order to create lasting change and a fundamental transformation of attitudes towards social irregularities, advocacy is needed.

Preventing human rights violations through advocacy

We all have a voice, but not everyone knows how to use it. An advocate does more than just speak up - they encourage change-makers and educate them on the issues at hand so that their voices can be heard too. Those who are advocates for change don't just show up and ask questions. They work with the people in charge, listening closely before pointing out errors or calling out issues that need change. A true advocate will serve not just as a vocal protester but would go one step further by encouraging these changes through education instead of merely telling government leaders why something needs fixing (which happens quite frequently). To become an advocate, one simply needs more knowledge about the issue they are advocating for. To be an effective advocate, however, you need more than just knowledge. Excellent communication skills and the ability to listen are also crucial for success in this field. You don't become an effective advocate overnight. It might take years of dedication to learn how the system works from the inside out before you're ready and have established authority. But every first step starts with action! If you've had a sudden change of heart while reading these lines and want to start taking action, keep reading for an easy way to become an advocate for your community, which can be implemented immediately.

Do you recall what I said above, quoting young advocate Ewa Lewis, that the first thing you have to do to become an advocate is learning how to listen? No matter where you are in the world, whether you're in the United States or in any country, your community needs your help. There is always a vulnerable group of people that requires support and their voices heard. So listen to their needs, listen to their stories…What do they need support with? Then represent those people and become their voice, talk with decision-makers, raise awareness among other community members, help educate...and don't forget to LISTEN!

Unfortunately, I've seen many young leaders sit at the negotiating table or meet with government officials and act as if they are entitled. They aren't open-minded enough to listen and assume they are up against something instead of looking for ways to find common ground before starting disputes over demands. Make no mistake assuming that all government officials oppose change and want human rights violations to happen; they often need help to see that change is necessary. Force has never been a good solution. Do not force your ideas on them, but instead communicate, educate them, offer solutions, ask them, 'What can I do to help you?'

Finally, one last recommendation, just as there is no Chef good at all, no advocate is good at everything. Don't be a jack of all trades master of none. You have to choose one topic first and master that. For example, if you are passionate about helping children, focus on children's rights advocacy first; if you want to help older people in need, focus on ending poverty for elders and so forth.

CHAPTER 4

HUMAN RIGHTS EDUCATION

———— ◆◇◆ ————

Promote peace with education

The human rights era is often traced to struggles against slavery and government oppression following World War I. Academics, advocates, leaders of organizations, activists, and citizens called for an international document to protect fundamental human rights and prevent future wars. Thus in 1919, the League of Nations was formed as an international organization that sought to promote peace and economic justice among its members. The goal was not just stopping one conflict but creating better conditions through building alliances across many nations so another World War doesn't occur (Houseden, 2014). However, the League of Nations had many weaknesses that eventually led to its downfall, in particular failing its primary goal of preventing another war from happening. World War II demonstrated the fragility of peace in international relations, and it was not until after this devastating war that a much more effective mechanism for maintaining peace and order among nations had been desired. After World War II there became clear that previous attempts had failed adequately enough. With this aim in mind, the United Nations was created in 1945 by 51 countries committed to preserving international peace. The UN Chapter adopted on June 26, 1945, restored faith in human rights and established an international agreement that worked to promote equality among men and women across nations, large or small. In order to create a more peaceful world, governments from all over have united and signed the Charter, which expresses their common ideals:

> *We, the **peoples of the United Nations** determined to save succeeding generations from the scourge of war, which twice in our lifetime has brought untold sorrow to mankind, and **to reaffirm faith in fundamental human rights**, in the dignity and worth of the human person, **in the equal rights of men and women** and of nations large and small, and to establish conditions under which justice and respect for the obligations arising from treaties and other sources of international law can be maintained, and **to promote social progress and better standards of life** in larger freedom...*
>
> *Preamble, Charter of the United Nations*

Later, in 1948, The United Nations Universal Declaration on Human Rights (UDHR) came into effect, providing guidelines regarding how individuals should be treated within society. The dream of Eleanor Roosevelt and the drafters of the Declaration was that they should be taught everywhere, anywhere. In the end, how can you stand up or defend your rights if you don't know what they are? While the fight for the defense of human rights is essential, it should not be overlooked the means by which this fight can be prevented altogether. **And that is achieved through EDUCATION.**

The Preamble of the Universal Declaration of Human Rights itself proclaims that "every individual and every organ of society [...] shall strive by teaching and education to promote respect for these rights and freedoms." Therefore, the real intention behind the declaration was, first of all, to promote knowledge and understanding of human rights - **thus, Human Rights Education.** Human rights are based on the principle of respect for the individual. What human rights teach you is not only to defend your own rights but also to respect other people's rights. Because your right ends where the rights of others begin, only through human rights education can we give due importance to these rights and remind ourselves why they must not be neglected.

Empower the youth

A resilient, democratic society as we live in nowadays needs more than just conflicts and finger-pointing. We need solutions. After over a decade of working as a human rights advocate, I have come to understand that we can do more by educating people about their human rights. Always start from a small community to effect change in different countries. That's one common mistake that I've seen people make when they begin their journey into human rights advocacy. They have a passion for impacting millions but want to start with 1 million people at a time. It is like everything else in life; you don't advance to the university level unless you've first done elementary school.

When I started my work in human rights advocacy, I didn't start at the United Nations or at the White House or going to meet with diplomats and government officials as I do now. Human rights education begins at the grassroots level, teaching your friends, your family, your neighborhood, your classmates at school, and then others. I started with my school. At that time, I was doing my Masters in Law at the University of Buffalo, and one day I got the idea to inspire all my colleagues to pledge for gender equality. In honor of International Women's Day, I put together "an event" in the law school's hallway. It was basically a table with a sign, some pens, and paper. At that time, I was just a few months into my Master's program when I realized that nobody was planning to address women's rights on International Women's Day. Like it didn't even exist. So I refused to be a bystander. I went above and beyond to get the school's administration approval to create an ad-hoc event overnight. To understand the issue's complexity, I had only one weekend to get the approvals from school, prepare all logistics, send out invitations, come up with the right theme, and host the event. And I was by myself. There was no time to get anyone on board. It was only one man's effort (or woman in my case). Still, I decided that I was going to do it. I created the event as wanted and managed to raise awareness through students and professors that gender equality matters. Not only that, but my event went viral on social media in just a few hours. Soon, students, professors, faculty administrators, the Dean, and everyone was on board, signing pledges and raising awareness on gender equality.

But that only ignited my passion. I desired to implement human rights education in my city and used my skills to speak about the importance of respecting others. I started delivering free presentations, workshops, and seminars to students from university-level to all age groups - including 8-year-olds! Students came up to their teacher after my workshop or during lunchtime, opening up about home abuse from siblings, parents, or family members. One time right after class, a 10-year old approached me, thanking me for opening his eyes to some issues like bullying because he now understands why specific actions were hurting his classmates and were wrong. And that was not me telling them they were wrong or that they shouldn't bully their classmates. That was a child's own intuitive grasp of reality through education. From the perspective of a 10-year-old student who has never been allowed any freedom or individuality before then - nor does he have many friends his own age--an understanding and knowledge about what our society expects from us can be empowering stuff!

When you work with children, and you educate them as to what their human rights are, you see a drop in bullying. In fact, according to UNESCO, one-third of the globe's youth is bullied (UNESCO, 2018). However, research shows that when a bystander intervenes, the bullied student will stop being hurt within 10 seconds 57 percent of the time (Espalage, 2012). Teaching youth about human rights will not only inspire them not to get involved in bullying themselves but also speak up when they see disrespect for another person's right. When kids have the knowledge of the rights they have, ALL of the rights that they have, they start to understand that other people around them have these rights too. They begin to treat each other differently, and they start to see themselves differently. I've taught kids in schools, students, community leaders, and even government officials, and I was able to see change when human rights education was implemented. There are many programs out there in our communities, and I am sure you are all familiar with a few of them that say: STAND UP FOR YOUR RIGHTS. The problem is if you don't know what your rights are, and you don't know what the rights of others around you are, **HOW WILL YOU KNOW WHEN TO STAND UP?**

Human Rights Education Case Studies

There are not many studies in the literature on the impact that human rights education can have on young people, and very few have come to show their value. Human rights are the key to a developed human society. This is due to their global impact because they really are the basis of everything a country needs - from its policies to its education systems, national action plans, and economic development strategies.

Bajaj et al. (2017) conducted a revealing ethnographic case study that assessed the impact of human rights education among immigrant and refugee youth. Their research provides excellent insight on how youth view human rights and how education about rights can aid in the process of their self-making (Bajaj et al., 2017). The study took place in the United States, where the researchers created an after-school human rights club at a public high school in Oakland, California. Over a period of two years, they've engaged with participants, particularly youth immigrants, collecting data through observation, interviews, and focus groups on how immigrant and refugee youths are impacted after receiving education about human rights during their participation in the human rights club. The study offers insights on how perspectives change after gaining more education about human rights in school and argues that human rights education has had a positive impact on the process of self-making and aided students in understanding more about their unique immigrant situations (Bajaj, 2017). A few years before this study, Monisha Bajaj traveled to India to conduct a complete study on the rise and impact of human rights education there. The journey and results are compiled in a book called "Schooling for Social Change," which presents data collected over a period of 13 months of research in India (Bajaj, 2011). She examined different conceptualizations of human rights education, engaging in qualitative research and conducting interviews, organizing focus groups, observing human rights teacher interactions in class and human rights summer camps, and participants. In total, she visited 60 schools and 6 NGOs all throughout India. Using survey data, Bajaj compares student responses from schools with human rights education intervention with those who did not have education and argues that human rights education can take multiple forms, from grassroots movements to school interactions (Bajaj, 2011).

Another case study in the field of human rights education is that of Covell and Howe that analyzed children's rights education in Canada (Covell and Howe, 1999). The authors argue that an essential means to make children aware of the human rights conventions (and indirectly adults) is through education (Covell and Howe, 1999). To assess the impact of human rights education on children, they've designed a curriculum explaining rights, which they offered to teachers. Then, they interviewed the children who have been taught the curriculum over a period of a school year. To evaluate the impact of the curriculum, the researchers created several scales to which they assigned scores. One scale measured the children's beliefs on accepting other classmates who have differences (e.g., African-Canadian, Native, in a wheelchair, or middle-class white) (Covell and Howe, 1999). Different scales measured the children's group membership' acceptance or teacher and peer support. The results showed that "children who received the curriculum had a broader and more accurate knowledge of children's rights compared to children who did not receive the curriculum" (Covell and Howe, 1999).

Ramirez et al. argue that human rights education movements create a global impact (Ramirez et al., 2007). They analyze statistics about human rights education internationally and released by the International Bureau of Education and show that from 160 countries, over 49 countries mention human rights in their national reports on education, and 86 countries reported to the UN High Commissioner for Human Rights their human rights education activities.

Finally, focusing on the African continent, Simmonds and Du Prezz bring forth the different discourses about human rights education from inception to growth and cynicism (Simmonds and Du Prezz, 2017). The researchers review the Constitution and Bill of Rights of South Africa, a series of documents and reports on human rights and education, as well as several doctoral theses by scholars that discuss human rights education and argue that human rights education research is "predominantly school-based" and "fundamentally descriptive and uncritical" (Simmonds and Du Prezz, 2017).

CHAPTER 5

CREATING LEADERSHIP THROUGH NGO ADVOCACY

———— ◆◇◆ ————

Becoming an NGO leader

What does it take to be a successful leader of an NGO? How do you rise to the top and make a real difference in the world? These are questions that many young people aspire to answer. And while there is no one-size-fits-all answer, there are a few things that can help you on your way. So if you're interested in making a difference in the world, keep reading! We'll explore what it takes to be an NGO leader and share some tips for success.

In the previous chapter, you saw that the demand for human rights education is vast and growing. Human rights education is a vital and necessary tool for human rights advocates. Yet, it can be difficult to reach larger groups of people beyond the community level when you're just one individual. That is one of the main complaints I hear from my students taking the Human rights training course and other advocates I meet from around the world, and I agree. Sometimes it's difficult to reach larger groups beyond the community level when you're just one individual. Many human rights advocates understand the importance of education and the impact that it can have, but it's clear that more needs to be done. For these reasons, driven advocates prefer partnering with nonprofit organizations or creating their own NGO so that they can exponentially increase their impact beyond physical borders. Typically because they feel they can be more effective in their human rights work if they are supported by an organization that can provide them with resources and volunteers. Indeed, a nonprofit can greatly expand advocacy due to its capacity to bring like-minded individuals together for a mutual cause. For these reasons, I chose to include this important chapter in my book to provide you with a brief overview, from my own perspective – as a human rights advocate and leader of an NGO, what it takes to become an NGO leader. I'm going to explain what NGOs are, why they are needed in today's society, and finally address the most significant question there is - How do I create my own NGO? By the end, you'll have a good understanding of what NGOs are and how they can help you spread your mission in human rights advocacy.

What is an NGO?

What is an NGO? This is a question that people of all ages might ask. NGOs, or non-governmental organizations, can be challenging to define. In 1945, the Charter of the newly formed United Nations was established in Article 71, non-governmental organizations, or NGOs (U.N. Charter).

These entities are independent and not-for-profit (WHO, 2016). They can be many different things to many other people. In general, however, an NGO is an organization that is neither a part of the government nor a for-profit company. Instead, it is run by volunteers or private citizens who are driven by a mission to help others. There are thousands of NGOs worldwide, and each one has its own unique purpose and agenda. Whether they're fighting for human rights, working to improve education or health care, or trying to protect the environment, these groups make a significant impact on our world. So what makes an NGO so unique? The answer lies not only within their mission or vision but also by who runs them, the people that make up this group, and how they operate together as one body to accomplish goals set forth through volunteering time and energy.

NGOs are non-state actors, meaning they are not controlled by a government. After the Second World War and especially after the creation of the United Nations, the global scene showed a significant increase in the number of non-state actors involved in global governance. NGOs have been vital gateways to information from a grassroots level, which would otherwise be difficult or impossible for outsiders. Their flexible organizational structure and lack of bureaucracy - typical in state institutions - allows them to respond and provide immediate support when needed quickly. For example, NGOs have become preferred methods of providing disaster relief in affected areas, and frequently even governments use them to provide humanitarian aid to those in need.

The need for NGOs

Non-governmental organizations fill a critical role in society by providing valuable services that governments may not always be able to deliver. From poverty relief to human rights advocacy, NGOs are vital for supporting the most vulnerable members of our communities. NGOs are an integral part of society and are involved globally in human rights, climate change, and humanitarian aid. When it comes to women's rights, the achievements made in terms of reproductive health and empowerment were initiated by international NGOs (Joachim 2003, 247). Some scholars even believe that the information provided by NGOs is more reliable than that of state actors (Keck and Sikkink 1998, 36). When it comes to international treaties, human rights NGOs are a powerful force. Hathaway's (2007) research showed the effect that NGOs have on ratification of international conventions, arguing that "for each ten additional human rights NGOs located in the state, the state has an increased chance of ratifying" (Hathaway 2007, 609). NGOs have been a driving force in establishing international norms. Lake (2010) states that the most obvious place for this is human rights, where NGOs create strong norms regarding civil and political rights (Lake 2010, 599). There are many ways in which NGOs persuade governments to adopt human rights-related legislation. Some of these include organizing protests and demonstrations, providing information for the general public through exhibits, side events, and formal speeches, or lobbying officials during meetings and negotiations (Rietig 2016, 270). For example, organizations such as CARE and Save the Children have conducted many campaigns to oppose legislation by the

United States government that affects children (Lall 2017, 276). Moreover, the UN Office of the High Commissioner for Human Rights provides funding for NGOs. It encourages them to submit shadow reports presenting alternative information to that of states on the situation of human rights in a specific country (Goodman and Jinks 2003, 177).

NGOs are often thought of as the "good guys." They provide essential services to people who need them, they advocate for human rights, and they fill a critical role in society. However, because NGOs are not government actors, they do not always have the same rights and protections that states enjoy. This can make it difficult for NGOs to operate in some countries. Despite their evolving nature, NGOs should be given an equal footing in international law. This would entail granting them the same rights as state actors and IGOs, while also acknowledging their essential role in global governance. Only through further study and clarification of NGO status can we hope to give these vital actors the recognition they deserve. Only then can we say that we have a clear understanding of the role NGOs play in our increasingly complex world.

Creating your own NGO

There are many reasons someone might choose to start their own non-governmental organization. Perhaps they feel passionate about a particular issue and want to use their skills and talents to make a difference. Or maybe they've been affected by one specific problem and want to create the conditions so that other people don't have to go through the same problem again. Around the world, people are faced with all sorts of issues. Many times, these problems seem too big or too complex for any one person to solve on their own. That's where non-governmental organizations come in. For starters, here are some of the benefits why starting an NGO is one of the best decisions you'll ever make:

1) You'll have a greater impact on the world.

2) You'll have more control over your life and career.

3) You'll be able to make a real difference in people's lives.

4) You'll gain invaluable experience and skills that will help you expand your cause and connect with like-minded people.

However, before being able to experience all these benefits, there is one thing to think about before you start your own NGO. One of the most important questions that you need to ask yourself is – Why? Why do you want to create an NGO? What are your motivations for wanting to make a difference in the world? And it cannot be simply "I want to make a greater impact." As you've seen above, that will be one of the benefits of having that NGO. Think about what motivates you...What makes you get out of bed in the morning and keeps you going? I established my NGO with the purpose of giving vulnerable children an opportunity that they might otherwise be denied – an opportunity at education! So even when I feel sick, even when I feel like not getting out of bed in the morning (because we all have those days when we want nothing more than to hide from the world), I remind myself that I'm in this for a bigger purpose than myself. I remind myself that there are 258 million children out there who never went through primary schooling and are waiting on someone like me to give them an opportunity to fulfilling their dreams. There is no greater goal than giving these kids access to education. So you see...your Why, your motivation, has to be so strong that nothing can stop you in your mission. There are so many reasons why people might want to start an NGO, and each reason is valid in its own way. So, what's your motivation? Why do you want to start an NGO?

Once you have a clear mental picture of your Why, you can then start incorporating your NGO and make it official. Depending on your country, the legal procedures to create your own NGO might be different. The following are the most critical steps you need to follow, noting that this section is only meant as a guide and does not necessarily represent legal advice. As I mentioned, each country has its own legislation regarding NGOs, so I recommend that you familiarize yourself first with the procedures in your country and get expert legal advice. Here are the steps to create your own NGO:

1. Choose a Name for your NGO

What's in a name? Just about everything. When you're starting up your NGO, it's important to choose a name that resonates with your goals and mission and is also easy to remember. Avoid using phrases or words that people don't understand.

2. Perform an online search to ensure that there are no other organizations with the same name

The name you choose for your NGO needs to be something that is legally available and doesn't infringe on any other organizations' trademarks. You may not be able to get the name you want, but that doesn't mean it's gone forever. With every failed search and new idea, the though-the perfect match will soon find its way into view.

3. Prepare the Articles of Incorporation

The articles of incorporation are a crucial part of establishing the legal description for your organization. These documents are usually filed with the local government where your NGO is created, grant power to board members, and specify the organization's name, purpose, or mission statement as well as where it's located (city/state).

4. Choose your Board of Directors

Many websites out there tell you that when you're starting an NGO, the first thing you'll need is a board of directors. While it is true that the members of an NGO's board of directors play an essential role in its success, in practice, assembling the board and identifying the right people is not easy. When building a board, it takes time to find the right people. You need knowledge and skills, as well as relationships with various stakeholders for your organization's goals, to be met efficiently – which means that not only will you have spent months finding these individuals but also training them on what they need to do once hired. For these reasons, I added this as a fourth necessary step after you have already initiated the preparations for establishing your legal entity. The board then will help you further in setting up the organization's strategic direction, overseeing its operations, and making sure it complies with all applicable laws and regulations. In addition, they will act as ambassadors for the NGO and raise money to support its work.

5. Draft your Bylaws or Operating Agreement

In order to make sure your NGO runs smoothly, it's essential to have some basic bylaws in place. The bylaws are a set of rules that dictate how your NGO will operate. They can include things such as how many members will serve on your board, how often board meetings will be held, what time they will start, and who is allowed to vote on NGO decisions. Drafting up your own bylaws can seem like a daunting task, but luckily there are plenty of resources available to help you get started.

6. Set up any policies

These policies can be Ethical conduct codes, Conflict of Interest policies, Anti-discrimination policies, and any other corporate responsibility policies that you think fit your mission and purpose.

7. Register with the tax entity and obtain tax exemption

When starting your NGO, it is vital to make sure you are registered as a tax entity. This allows your NGO to receive donations and other payments without paying taxes on them. Talk with an accountant or a tax professional to help you with this step.

8. Set up your bank account

Now that the legal basis has been set, it is time to open up your NGO bank account. When you start your own NGO, you will need to set up a bank account for your organization. This will make it easier to track your expenses and keep your accounts organized.

9. Prepare agenda and minutes for the First meeting of the board

Minutes are a summarized recording of the proceedings at a meeting. They include a record of what was decided and who made the decisions. The First meeting of the board is an important milestone for your NGO.

10. Establish your online presence - website, social media, Google Maps

In order to be successful, non-governmental organizations (NGOs) need to have a robust online presence. This means having an effective website, using social media channels to reach your target audience, and ensuring your organization is listed on Google Maps.

11. Build your reputation within the community

When starting your own NGO, it is important to build a good reputation within the community. This means being involved in local events, working with other charities and organizations, and networking with people in your area. By doing this, you will create goodwill for your organization and make people more likely to support your work. It can also be helpful to have a solid social media presence, so people can learn more about your organization and what you are doing. By taking the time to build a good reputation, you will help ensure the success of your NGO.

CHAPTER 6

BECOMING A HUMAN RIGHTS CONSULTANT

———— ◆◇◆ ————

What is a Human Rights Consultant?

Let's start with addressing the elephant in the room. This is a question that I get asked frequently. What does the term "human rights consultant" mean, and why do people want to hire you for their projects? If this is the first time you're hearing about it, it's okay. I'll help make sense of this profession.

First, the human rights industry is an unregulated profession. That means there is no regulatory body overseeing the profession. With a simple search on career websites, you can find hundreds of jobs that require a human rights consultant, and most of them do not require individuals to have a law degree or be a lawyer. Why is that? Because a human rights consultant doesn't have to be a lawyer because they do not practice law. The human rights consultant's purpose is to teach people about human rights and help individuals and companies understand and promote human rights.

Human rights consultants don't just understand the problems that exist and affect the human rights of all; they also make a difference by bringing solutions and educating others. The human rights consultant goes beyond mere activism and is a true advocate for creating new policies that uphold human rights and prevent human rights violations from even happening in the first place. A human rights consultant does not go to court, take on clients to help them with complaints on human rights violations or any other similar activities that would be considered practicing law. A consultant's role is to listen and provide solutions.

Why do we have financial consultants, business consultants, IT consultants, management consultants, but not human rights consultants? You might not like replying with a question, but this will help you gain a conceptual understanding of the role and importance of a human rights consultant.

Do you go to a doctor or someone who is good at googling on WebMD? Why hire an accountant if all the information on how to do taxes is on the Internet? Why hire an interior designer if anyone can look on Pinterest how to decorate a house? Simple. Because there is a need for specialized knowledge in that field. Companies need specialists to help them draft human rights policies and protect their employees. Companies and individuals need training, oversight, and specialized knowledge. So, while it is true that information is readily available nowadays in any subject possible, would you trust such an important topic to be "researched" on the Internet where there is also misinformation, or would a company prefer to hire specialists who their entire life and job are about that information?

There are many talks these days about corporate social responsibility, and more and more businesses are looking to hire human rights consultants to help them ensure they are living up to their ethical standards. In the following, I'll present some benefits of working with a human rights consultant and outline some of the critical services they can provide:

- Consult on policies and procedures related to human rights compliance

- Advice on best practices for implementing human rights programs

- Assist with audits of operations against international standards

- Help develop training programs for employees.

- Research and help draft human rights-related policies on discrimination at work; harassment at work; diversity and inclusion; patient's rights, and others

- Advocate on behalf of the company

To be a human rights consultant is to have the duty of raising awareness of peoples' rights and providing solutions. The world needs more people with a commitment to human rights. The human rights consultant believes that an essential thing in human rights is based on the principle of respect for the individual. Human rights consultants work towards raising awareness and providing solutions, believing that the most critical thing in our species' right is based on moral grounds: each individual deserves respect no matter what they do or who they are.

At the US Institute of Diplomacy and Human Rights, through our Human Rights Consultant certification training, I have now trained and certified more than 3,500 human rights consultants that are now able to go out there and help thousands of other individuals and businesses understand the topic of human rights and implement human rights-related policies to improve the society, and the community we live in.

Conducting assessments for businesses and delivering training

As a human rights consultant, before taking on a new client, you should always conduct a training/policy need assessment. An assessment is the first step to any successful consultancy. The assessment's role is to identify individuals' current level of competency, skill, or knowledge in the field of human rights.

One question that I get asked quite often is who are the clients of a human rights consultant? A human rights consultant may work with various clients to protect and promote human rights. Some of these clients may include individuals, private companies, non-governmental organizations (NGOs), and government agencies. By working with a wide range of clients, a human rights consultant can better assess the needs of different groups and identify potential areas where human rights violations may occur. Additionally, by collaborating with NGOs and other civil society organizations, a human rights consultant can help raise awareness about critical human rights issues and advocate for change. Big corporates have budgets allocated every year toward human rights training. Other clients can include schools, hospitals, law enforcement, security personnel, TSA, hotel management and employees, all travel facilitators, small businesses, local government, basically anyone that works with people.

When you're taking on a new business client as a human rights consultant, besides listening to their wants and needs, conduct an assessment to understand where that company and its employees sit. To perform the evaluation, you should at minimum ask them the following questions:

- How much do participants know about human rights in general and human rights in the respective industry in particular?

- Have they attended previous training, workshops, or seminars?

- Are they aware of any existing national or international laws?

- Does the company have policies set in place? Does it offer pamphlets handbooks to newly hired employees explaining their rights and responsibilities?

- Does the company have a system of complaints or reports? Are employees encouraged to report human rights violations happening at work?

- What are the positions in the organization of each participant, and how could their work be affected by the lack of knowledge on the subject of human rights?

- Do employees know what to do if they encounter a suspicious case that might be a case of discrimination at work, harassment, or even human trafficking?

Evaluate the assessment you just did and build a tailored plan for your prospective client. Your project can recommend specific actions that the client needs to take (i.e., implementing specific policies) and training. In the following chapter, we will discuss specifically how to deliver human rights training.

CHAPTER 7

DELIVER HUMAN RIGHTS TRAINING

———— ◆◇◆ ————

Why are human rights trainings needed?

Think about all the different human rights violations that take place in the world. It can be overwhelming trying to think of what we could do to prevent them. One way to help is by delivering actual training on human rights in our schools and communities. The dream of the drafters of the Universal Declaration of Human Rights was to educate and teach everyone about their rights. The preamble of this document highlights that education about human rights is key to achieving respect for those principles. The emphasis isn't put on acknowledging that every individual has such a right, but rather the importance of respecting the rights of others, which can only be achieved by teaching and education:

> *"Proclaims this Universal Declaration of Human Rights as a common standard of achievement for all peoples and all nations, to the end that every individual and every organ of society, keeping this Declaration constantly in mind, shall strive **by teaching and education** to promote **respect** for these rights and freedoms and by progressive measures, national and international, to secure their universal and effective recognition and observance, both among the peoples of Member States themselves and among the peoples of territories under their jurisdiction."*
>
> **Preamble, Universal Declaration of Human Rights**

There are many reasons why human rights trainings are needed, but one of the most important is to raise awareness about what human rights are and how they can be protected. Without this knowledge, it can be difficult for individuals to stand up for their rights or the rights of others. Another reason why these trainings are so important is that they can help people learn how to spot and respond to human rights violations. By being alert to these potential abuses, we can work together to stop them from happening. Lastly, human rights trainings provide a space for open dialogue and collaboration on ways to improve human rights protection both locally and globally. By coming together to learn more about human rights, we can create a brighter future for everyone.

You've seen why it is essential for others to receive human rights training. But why do you need to deliver human rights training? By conducting human rights trainings, you can become an agent of change in your community. Every day people are subjected to human rights abuses. This can be anything from being verbally abused, having our rights violated at work or in public, or even experiencing violence or sexual assault. We can't always control when these things happen to us, but we can prepare people by teaching them about their human rights and how to stand up for them. That's where human rights training comes in. It teaches people what their rights are, how to identify when they're being violated, and how to speak up for them. Human rights training is essential for everyone – not just advocates or people who think they might experience human rights abuses. By teaching others about their rights and how to stand up for them, we can create a world where everyone understands and respects fundamental human rights.

What should a training include?

The first important aspect that you need to look at when creating your training is who your participants are. When designing human rights training, you should build an individual plan tailored to the specific group you're teaching. The goal of this process is to increase participants' awareness on the topic and make them leave your training with a certainty of what human rights are, what human rights do people have, how many human rights they have, where they can look for resources if they need more help. You should ask yourself at least these two questions:

- **What do my participants know about human rights?** How much knowledge do participants already have on the topic in general and their applicability in their respective industries? Have they attended previous training/workshops/seminars, or are they new to the topic?

- **Who are your participants, and what's their current role?** What type of job do they have? Are they in the products or service industry, or are they, students? What would happen if they were less informed about human rights issues? How will a lack of understanding affect their day-to-day from now onwards?

When you know who will be attending, it's a good idea to prepare in advance and customize your presentation. However, sometimes you'll only know general information about the participants (i.e., they are students, they are employees of an insurance company), in which case you must attempt to find out the answer to the above questions early in your presentation. Simply ask the questions to participants and select a few of them to answer.

The second most crucial aspect that you need to look at when creating your training is your available timeframe. How much available time do you have to deliver a training? The rule of thumb is: anything that is less than 3 hours is not a training but a presentation.

HOW TO BECOME A HUMAN RIGHTS PROFESSIONAL

At a minimum, you'll need 2.5 hours to deliver professional training, because a training usually includes the following:

- Ten minutes introduction

- Ten minutes orientation into the training

- Thirty minutes presentation

- Fifteen-minute break

- Five-minute discussions after each human right presented (Thirty minutes for five rights, for example)

- Twenty minutes Q&A

- Twenty minutes extra for handling unforeseen problems, such as technical issues, handing out materials, stopping to answer additional questions from participants.

Third, to create an effective human rights training program, it is crucial to include all the necessary components. Your human rights training should consist of at minimum the following:

1. Welcome and introduction

Tell a story about yourself. Why do you like human rights? How did you end up working in human rights? What is your expertise or background experience (i.e., you are the founder of an NGO; you are a nurse and have witnessed multiple human rights violations that made you want to stand up). Make sure you include personal details about what made you start your journey in this career and how you've already helped others. If you have, include any testimonials from previous training you've delivered.

2. Clarify the purpose of the training

Be straightforward about the objective of the training. Tell them what they can expect to learn from you.

Example: You can start by listing what they won't learn in this training: this training is not about filing complaints against human rights violations; we won't be covering all the available international human rights documents. Or what they will learn – Our purpose is that every person leaves today with a certainty of the 30 human rights that each have as well as a deeper understanding as to why each person's knowledge of their human rights is the key to everything we are looking to handle in society.

3. Clarify why the content of the training is relevant to them

The relevance of the training to the participants is essential to its success. The participants must see how the skills they are learning can be applied to their current or future profession. This way, they will be more likely to put forth the effort and contribute positively to the training.

Example: You're delivering a human rights training to school teachers. You'd be telling them: When you work with children, and you educate them as to what their human rights are, you'll see a drop in bullying. When kids have the knowledge of the rights they have, ALL of the rights that they have, they start to understand that other people around them have these rights too. They start to treat each other differently, and they start to see themselves differently.

4. Explain the structure of the training

Now that you established the main objectives and what they will learn or not learn in your presentation and also gave them an overview of why it is essential for them to get this knowledge, it is time to provide the participants with a basic overview or outline of how the training will be conducted and what it includes.

Example: In this 2-hour training, we will go over definitions of human rights and how they came to be. We will go over the significant milestones and international conventions that proclaim human rights. We will then analyze a few human rights listed in the Universal Declaration of Human Rights and discuss them along. We will see some case studies and give you practical examples to build a conceptual understanding of how these rights apply in day-to-day life. Then we will have a 15-minute break when you can take a sip of water, use the restroom, eat a snack. Then we will come back together in the class, and we will continue with part two of the training, in which we will pick other human rights and analyze them. In the end, we will have a 15-minute Q&A session where I will allow you to ask questions based on the information I've provided or other relevant questions.

5. Deliver the actual training

So, what would you include in your human rights training? It's a question with many answers, but the important thing is to ensure that all participants receive comprehensive and accurate information. **The key to delivering human rights is simplicity.** You should not try and deliver a Masters in Human Rights within the few hours that you have available, as it will only end up being confusing for those who are listening- either students or professionals already working with this subject matter. Your training needs more than just complicated jargon; instead, it is best if we can make our instructions simple enough so even children would understand them!

6. Wrap up and conclusions

What do participants think? Do they feel that their knowledge has expanded, or are they more confident about human rights issues? You could also go back to the initial questions you asked them, which may provide different perspectives on whether people now see themselves well-informed after this training. Name the objectives you had in mind at the beginning of the training. You should be able to tell whether or not you've achieved your aim by looking at the room. If they're all nodding in agreement, then it's likely that this goal has been met!

7. Call to action

This is a point that most people miss. Make sure you don't miss this opportunity. If you did a great job delivering the training, people would want to follow up with you. Maybe you have a book they can buy, or you have another more advanced course they can do. This is your moment to tell them what do you want them to do next? If you don't have another training or a book, then you can ask for feedback. Ask them to give you testimonials. Take written and video testimonials if possible. You'll then use them for the next group of participants and to attract more clients. But in any case, you don't want to miss this vital step.

8. Q&A session

Allow participants to address any questions they had prior to this training or that came up during this training. You should also have a few questions prepared in advance for this part that you can use to test whether they've assimilated the knowledge that you provided them with.

CHAPTER 8

HELP SHAPE HUMAN RIGHTS LEGISLATION

—— ◆◇◆ ——

Legislative advocacy

Human rights advocates play an important role in helping to shape human rights-related legislation. They can provide information about the effects of a proposed bill and voice the opinions of those who will be affected by it. Advocates can also build support for or against the law and help legislators understand the issues involved from a different perspective. In order to achieve the goals of human rights, people must work together with government representatives. This collaboration can take many various forms and involve both pressing issues like supporting bills or policies which affect your community, as well addressing problems within laws already enacted where there were unforeseen consequences due to citizen participation being overlooked during the drafting process. Legislative advocacy is different than activism. Effective advocacy includes you acting as a liaison between the government and the community and therefore is two-folded: you help the government by providing them with valuable information on the effects that specific laws could have, and you represent the voice of the people ensuring that policies and laws are developed with consideration of their rights. Working on legislative advocacy in the field of human rights means several things:

- Proposing new legislation to be enacted

- Working on passing human rights legislation

- Working on changing/modifying current legislation that affects people's rights

Proposing new legislation to be enacted: many people assume that they are already protected under the law. Unfortunately, not all countries have strong human rights laws in place, which can lead to serious abuses. In light of this, the community and human rights advocates have come together to propose new human rights legislation. For example, proposing legislation on how to combat human trafficking in your area, how to prevent discrimination at work, how to provide protections for the LGBTQ+ community, how to promote religious freedom and to avoid hatred based on faith, etc.

Help pass human rights legislation: someone else, be it legislator or a community member, has already had the initiative of drafting a law that promotes a human rights-related issue. You can join forces and help raise awareness on their behalf on the existence of that law; show your support to the legislator sponsoring that bill by emailing them or visiting them at their office, as well as providing them with feedback; contact other legislators and help them see the benefits of having that bill enacted and express your opinion. Have you ever wondered why some policies work well and others don't? It is because they lack citizen participation. When advocates are engaged in the process, they can provide public comments on laws that help legislators understand different perspectives.

Changing current legislation: one other way you can advocate for change is by influencing your state government. There are many pieces of legislation that affect people's rights, and it's vital that we voice our concerns to our legislators. Often, we can make a difference simply by speaking up and letting our elected officials know where we stand on an issue. Whether you're an expert or not, your insight on the local impact of a specific law can help elected officials understand which policies work and which have negative implications for specific categories of people. For example, an immigration bill that increases the time that children who arrive at the border be kept in custody from 20 to 100 days has a severe impact on children's well-being was vehemently opposed by Save the Children in 2019.

Case studies

One of the areas of politics that can be particularly confusing for newcomers is legislative advocacy. What is it? How do I do it? And most importantly, why should I even bother? In the world of politics, there are a million things going on at once. It can be hard to keep up, especially if you don't know where to start. When you're first introduced to the concept of legislative advocacy, it can seem daunting. If this is the first time you're reading about it, you might think this is such a hard thing to do. After all, lawmakers are busy people, and they likely won't have time to listen to your concerns. However, becoming familiar with the basics of how to interact with legislators is something that just about anyone can do with a bit of effort. And the best way to explain it to you is by leading with the power of example.

In 2017-2018, legislators, NGOs, civil society, and advocates worked together to convince the U.S. Congress and Senate to adopt two essential bills impacting human trafficking; these are known as FOSTA - Fight Online Sex Trafficking Act (FOSTA), and its companion bill "The Stop Enabling Sex traffickers Act" or SESTA...As the names suggest, the bills aimed at combatting human trafficking online. With the advancements in the IoT (Internet of Things) sector, the Internet opened up new avenues for criminals to target victims who would come with innovative ways to commit crimes online.

HOW TO BECOME A HUMAN RIGHTS PROFESSIONAL

The above bills aimed to solve the problem of online trafficking in persons, targeting free listing websites like Craigslist, Backpage, and other free listing websites that have previously provided a safe haven for sex workers. The bills were targeting these platforms because they didn't regulate the online space enough to prevent exploitation or help identify victims of human trafficking before it was too late. Some websites even offered tools to help sex workers vet potential clients — including shared blacklists for dangerous clients. These websites were a chance to move negotiations that occur on the street into an online space (Tung 2020). But no one was held accountable. The sites where the ads were posted won't take any responsibility arguing that they won't censor their customers and take down their advertisements. Users could post whatever they wanted as their identity was protected by privacy laws. Some websites simply were not taking any action to prevent the exploitation of victims; others, like Backpage.com, were knowingly allowing human trafficking to happen on their platform.

Here's an example of an advertisement found on one of these websites, from the testimony of a survivor of human trafficking:

> "The ads would start with whatever name I was given for the day [...]. It would describe my measurements — so my bust size, my hip size, my pant size, and my bra size. It would describe my race, and sometimes we decided to either — because I'm mixed race, so we decided to either stick with one of my races or both of them,

try to capitalize on that — and then it was some type of advertisement, something along the lines of, you know, 'I'll show you a good time,' 'I'm new in town,' any of these things that we knew sex buyers would gravitate towards." (Tung 2020)

But even though many people were in favor of taking on these big websites, the backlash from them was huge. Human traffickers didn't care about their victims, and activists had opposed government involvement in how sites are maintained because it would lead to more regulations for online content creators, which some argued could hurt free speech protections rather than protect them. The journey was not easy at all. Legislators were open to hearing debates from both sides and balancing the advantages and disadvantages of passing legislation that would hurt the industry so badly. At the same time, some sex workers were opposing the bills arguing that this would further put their lives in danger as they could no longer depend on the internet infrastructure.

It took more than a year of lobbying the government, meeting with stakeholders, hearing arguments on all sides, fighting for the victims to come to a result finally. And on March 23rd, before even the laws passed, Craigslist was the first one to take action by shutting down their "Personal" category, followed by other platforms such as Reddit, which amended its policies to explicitly forbid solicitation or facilitation of "paid services involving physical, sexual contact." Then, on April 6th, I remember that day as it was yesterday...my co-worker came into the office screaming with joy, asked me to pull up the news on my computer, and I saw this:

backpage.com and affiliated websites have been seized

as part of an enforcement action by the Federal Bureau of Investigation, the U.S. Postal Inspection Service, and the Internal Revenue Service Criminal Investigation Division, with analytical assistance from the Joint Regional Intelligence Center.

Other agencies participating in and supporting the enforcement action include the U.S. Attorney's Office for the District of Arizona, the U.S. Department of Justice's Child Exploitation and Obscenity Section, the U.S. Attorney's Office for the Central District of California, the office of the California Attorney General, and the office of the Texas Attorney General.

Additional information will be provided at around 6:00 pm EST on Friday, April 6, by the U.S. Department of Justice, and all media inquiries should be directed to the U.S. Department of Justice's Office of Public Affairs at 202-514-2007 and press@usdoj.gov.

April 6, 2018

I cried that day, knowing that I made a difference!

Federal law enforcement agencies have raided the office and house of its co-founder in what some are calling a two-year Senate investigation into online sex trafficking. Backpage knew they were aiding criminal activity, but it didn't stop them from making money off these ads that led women into slavery, according to investigators with The National Center for Missing & Exploited Children (NCMEC). I am so grateful and honored to have been one of the advocates working hard behind the scenes to help these laws become a reality. On April 11th, 2018, the FOSTA-SESTA bills were signed into law by President Trump.

CONCLUSION

As a youth participant, speaker, and organizer of many conferences, I have been asked most often, "How do you start working in human rights?" A lot of young professionals are looking for ways they can make an impact on the world. The best way may not always involve working for someone else or even traditional school - it could just come down to having passion about something that interests them enough where their drive and motivation comes from within instead of external forces pushing them around. The road to human rights advocacy is different than what you might have imagined. You learned that education about the topic could open doors previously unthought-of, and it's possible for someone like yourself with a calling in this area of work to create change within the community by helping others get more educated about human rights. Human rights don't teach you that you have rights, but that other people have rights too! Human rights are based on the principle of respect for the individual and your rights end where the rights of other people begin. If you understood at least that by reading this book, my work of helping you step into this profession is half done.

Then you learned that there are so many opportunities out there if you become a human rights consultant. And I am not talking only about getting a well-paid job as a consultant, but you can open your own NGO to impact millions and create leadership through your work in human rights advocacy. In Chapter 1, you discovered that what you need the most is to have a calling and tons of preparation. Not a law degree or special licenses. Without being hypocritical because I've followed that path – I got my law degree and masters in human rights law, but I find it absurd to have to go to law school and get a master's degree in the 21st Century to learn about your human rights. Even the Preamble of the Universal Declaration of Human Rights encourages teaching and education and the drafters' intention was to have this declaration taught in every school on Earth. But even seven decades after it was adopted, that dream did not come true.

This book is a guide for those who want to make change happen. I am writing this book so as to inspire you to take the lead and don't wait for governments, the United Nations, or someone else to do the work that you can do! If I had this book as a guide when I started my human rights journey, I could have done much more and faster. I would have loved to learn all these steps from someone who has gone through this to quickly turn me from a human rights leader into a true professional. But it took me years of working in the field, money spent on degrees and lots of courage to understand human rights as I do today. But you don't have to go through that. This book outlines the journey you need to take one step at a time. You don't become a human rights professional overnight, but it is also not hard to become one if you get into the footsteps of those who've done that dance already.

You may feel overwhelmed right now. This book is not a light reading, but if you're concerned about how to remember all the steps we just went over, then have no worries! You don't need to memorize anything because this was meant as a guide for easy referral when on the go. So make sure you carry it around and I can guarantee that will help handle unexpected situations better than ever before with instant results. Go back through these chapters frequently and refer where needed.

And if you've already decided that human rights is your calling and wish to go a step further, establish your authority faster in the field and learn all about delivering human rights training to others, I recommend you to **take the Human Rights Consultant training** with the US Institute of Diplomacy and Human Rights. With this training program, you can become a certified consultant in this vital field. We've already trained more than 3,500 consultants as of this date and they have gone on to impact millions of others. I created a special discounted link for you so that you can enroll at a fraction of its real cost:

→. https://usa.usidhr.org/humanrights

As you finish this book, I hope you have enjoyed the journey as much as I have. This has been a labor of love for me, and I am grateful to all of you who have taken the time to read it.

Thank you! Now, it's time to put this book away and start building your dream.

Isabelle Vladoiu

YOU MIGHT ALSO LIKE

Get the Business Etiquette Secrets Book at
https://usa.usidhr.org/book

BIBLIOGRAPHY

Bajaj, Monisha. (2011). Schooling for Social Change: The Rise and Impact of Human Rights Education in India. A&C Black.

Bajaj, M., Canlas, M. and Argenal, A., (2017). Between rights and realities: Human rights education for immigrant and refugee youth in an urban public high school. *Anthropology & Education Quarterly, 48*(2), pp.124-140.

Cambridge Advanced Learner's Dictionary & Thesaurus (2022) https://dictionary.cambridge.org/dictionary/english/advocacy Date accessed [13.02.22].

Charter of the United Nations., (1945) https://www.un.org/en/about-us/un-charter/full-text Date Accessed [13.02.22].

Covell, Katherine, and R. Brian Howe. (1999) The Impact of Children's Rights Education: A Canadian Study. *International Journal of Children's Rights* 7, no. 2: 171–84.

Declaration of the Rights of Man and of the Citizen of 1789 (French: Déclaration des Droits de l'Homme et du Citoyen de 1789). https://www.legifrance.gouv.fr/Droit-francais/Constitution/Declaration-des-Droits-de-l-Homme-et-du-Citoyen-de-1789 Date Accessed [13.02.22].

Domino, J.C., (2018). *Civil rights and liberties in the 21st century*. Routledge.

Donnelly, J., (2013). Universal human rights in theory and practice. Cornell University Press.

Espalage, D., Pigott, T., Polanin, J. (2012) "A Meta Analysis of School-Based Bullying Prevention Programs' Effects on Bystander Intervention Behavior." School Psychology Review, Volume 41, No. 1, 47–65.

Fassin, D., (2002). L'invention française de la discrimination. *Revue française de science politique, 52*(4), pp.403-423.

Holt, J. C. (1992). Magna Carta. Cambridge: Cambridge University Press.

Housden, M., (2014). The League of Nations and the Organization of Peace. Routledge.

Magna Carta (1297) *Translation*. National Archives and Records Administration. https://www.archives.gov/files/press/press-kits/magna-carta/magna-carta-translation.pdf Date Accessed [13.02.22].

Mason, G. (1776) The Virginia Declaration of Rights https://www.americanbar.org/content/dam/aba/migrated/2011_build/human_rights/virginia_declaration.pdf Date Accessed [13.02.22].

N.M.Vladoiu, O. Predescu., (2014). Drept european și internațional al drepturilor omului, Ed. Hamangiu, București.

Ramirez, F.O., Suárez, D. and Meyer, J.W., (2007). The worldwide rise of human rights education. In School knowledge in comparative and historical perspective (pp. 35-52). Springer, Dordrecht.

Roosevelt, E. (1948) The Struggle for Human Rights, Paris, France. https://etc.usf.edu/lit2go/185/civil-rights-and-conflict-in-the-united-states-selected-speeches/4853/the-struggle-for-human-rights-paris-france-september-28-1948/ Date Accessed [13.02.22].

Rousseau, J.J., (1964). The social contract (1762). London

Save the Children (2019). SCAN CEO Speaks Out Against Senate Bill To Be Introduced Tomorrow https://www.savethechildren.org/us/about-us/media-and-news/2019-press-releases/scan-ceo-speaks-out-against-senate-bill Date Accessed [13.02.22].

Sepuldeva, M., Van Banning, T., Gudmundsdóttir, G., Chamoun, C. and Van Genugten, W.J., (2010). Human rights reference handbook. University for Peace.

Simmonds, S. and Du Preez, P., (2017). Discourses shaping human rights education research in South Africa: Future considerations. South African Journal of Higher Education, 31(6), pp.9-24.

Simmons, A.J., (2020). The Lockean theory of rights. Princeton University Press.

The Bill of Rights. (1761) https://www.archives.gov/files/legislative/resources/education/bill-of-rights/images/handout-3.pdf Date Accessed [13.02.22].

The Declaration of Independence of the United States of America, (1776).
https://www.constitution.org/us_doi.pdf Date Accessed [13.02.2022].

UNESCO (2018) New SDG 4 Data on Bullying.
http://uis.unesco.org/en/news/new-sdg-4-data-bullying Date Accessed [13.02.22].

United Nations (2015) History of the UN https://www.un.org/un70/en/content/history/index.html Date Accessed [13.02.22].

United Nations (2022) Human Rights https://www.un.org/en/global-issues/human-rights Date Accessed [13.02.22].

World Health Organisation (2016) Framework of Engagement with Non-State Actors. https://www.who.int/about/collaborations/non-state-actors/A69_R10-FENSA-en.pdf#page=6&zoom=page-fit,-500,842 Date Accessed [13.02.22].